SPECIAL FRIENDS
OF JESUS
New Testament Stories

Written by Francine M. O'Connor
Illustrated by Kathryn Boswell

Catechetical Advisors: Redemptorist Fathers

LIGUORI
PUBLICATIONS

One Liguori Drive
Liguori, Missouri 63057
(314) 464-2500

Imprimi Potest:
John F. Dowd, C.SS.R.
Provincial, St. Louis Province
Redemptorist Fathers

Imprimatur:
+ Edward J. O'Donnell
Vicar General, Archdiocese of St. Louis

ISBN 0-89243-255-1
Library of Congress Catalog Card Number: 86-81411

Cover illustration from
The Friends of Jesus for Children
Regina Press, 1977

Table of Contents

Introduction

When Jesus entered our world, he did it in a remarkable way. The Incarnation transformed humanity into divinity, the ordinary into the extraordinary. The friends Jesus chose here on earth were people much like you and me. They had faults to be erased, weaknesses to be healed, human attitudes to be replaced by divine certainties. As Jesus effected these changes for those who walked with him, so, too, our remembrances of them should effect changes in our lives.

Children need to be led to the realization that every friendship Jesus had on earth was similar to their own friendship with him today. The lessons he taught, the forgiveness and love he offered, all these have been immortalized and carried personally into the children's own world. These little stories will help them to identify with the people of New Testament times and they will grow in spirituality through that identification. At the same time, it can be hoped that they will find in them a bit of fun and enjoyment for storytime.

— FMO

The Birth
of
Baby John

Somewhere in the hills beyond Galilee
lived a kindly old man and his wife.
His sweet lady fair
  with her silvery hair
was Elizabeth, the joy of his life.

The gentle old man was Zechariah,
a faithful, loving servant of God.
The two lived alone
    in a small mountain home
and they prayed many prayers for a child.

One day when Zechariah was praying,
God's angel appeared before his eyes.
Shimmering so bright
   with pure heavenly light,
the angel had a message of great surprise.

"You will have a baby son," the angel said.
But Zechariah just turned his face away.
"After all of these years
    and all of our tears,
I just can't believe the words you say."

9

God's angel had told his message true
and old Elizabeth gave birth to a son.
They named him John,
    which means "chosen one,"
and the baby brought cheer to their home.

Zechariah and Elizabeth said, "Thank you, Lord,
for the wonderful thing that you have done.
You filled us with joy
    when you gave us our boy,
and we know John will be a special son."

11

John was a joy to his mom and his dad,
but the very best part was still to come.
For one day their child
   would live in the wild
and announce the Good News about God's Son.

Like John, you are very special to God.
Someday you will know of his plan for you.
He will open your eyes
    to a wonderful surprise,
for your love is strong and your heart is true.

The Lady and the Angel

This is the story of MARY,
the beautiful lady from Nazareth
who talked to an angel named Gabriel
on the quietest of quiet nights
when God's Word was brought to our world.

And the angel called her BLESSED,
because she was chosen by God himself.
Out of all the lovely young maidens
who lived in the world he had made,
God chose this very special one
to give birth to Jesus, his only Son.

And Jesus called her MOTHER.
When he was the tiniest boy
she gave him every bit of her love.

She held his hand as he learned to walk
and kissed his bruises when he fell down.
And once, when he was out of her sight,
she worred until she found him —
then scolded him for giving her such a fright.

17

And we call her OUR LADY
because Jesus told her to watch over us.
For he knows how well she understands
about skinned knees and broken toys
and temper tantrums when we are tired
and the loneliness of being small
in a world that is very, very big.

The Man in the Desert

John, John, Elizabeth's son,
dressed in a camel's hair robe.
He lived in the desert and ate strange food
and announced the Word of the Lord.

The people came from miles around
just to listen to Elizabeth's son.
They would step down into the river
to be baptized there by John.

"Someone special is coming soon,"
was the Baptizer's happy shout.
Now read each clue to see if you
can guess who John is talking about.

John's special Someone
   comes from God.
He was born on the first
   Christmas day.

The blind will see
   and the lame will walk
when this Someone
   comes their way.

He'll choose twelve men
   to follow him.
He'll speak of heaven,
   from whence he came.

They'll learn to pray
   his special prayer
"Our Father . . .
   hallowed be thy name."

He'll make a loaves-
   and-fishes feast
for the thousands
   who listen to him.

He'll die for the love
   of you and me
. . . then rise and never
   die again.

Do you know who this Someone is?
It's a secret God told to John.
When that special One was baptized
God said, "THIS IS MY BELOVED SON."

The Twelve Who Walked with Jesus

Jesus is calling his special helpers
to come and work with him every day.
They will follow him from town to town
and listen to all that he has to say.

Andrew and his big brother, Peter,
are mending their nets by the sea.
Jesus calls for them to come:
"Come be fishers of men," says he.

He calls two brothers, James and John,
the "Sons of the Thunder," to be his own.
And Philip and Thomas, the doubting one,
join the working team of God's own Son.

Now he calls Levi, the tax collector.
(The people really don't like this man.)
But Jesus has dinner at Levi's house
and Levi becomes Matthew, Jesus' friend.

He calls Simon, known as "the Zealot,"
and the one they all call Bartholomew.
Two Judases plus a James make twelve,
and all except one remain loyal and true.

Today Jesus' friends are too many to count.
All over the world they follow his way.
And YOU are his very best friend of all,
for you keep his love in your heart every day.

Always walk the way that Jesus walked,
remain his best friend, loyal and true.
Remember the Father's special love
and heaven, where Jesus is waiting for you.

The Fishermen's Story

Simon was a fisherman, powerful and strong.
And Andrew, his brother, was a fisherman too.
The two would go out in the dark of the night
and have their nets filled with fish before dawn.

Families would stand on the shores of the lake
to welcome men home at the break of the day.
When Simon and Andrew came into view
the people would cheer the team on its way.

One night they fished until the sun came up,
but not even a minnow would swim their way.
They pulled into shore, empty-handed and tired,
and started to wash out their nets for the day.

Jesus strolled by and came down to the lake.
And behind him there was a great crowd.
Jesus climbed in the boat, pulled out from shore,
then began to teach the crowd about God.

When his teaching was done, Jesus spoke to Simon:
"Put out into deep waters and lower your net."
"We've been at it all night," Simon explained,
"and we have not caught a single fish yet."

But Simon did exactly what Jesus had asked,
for Jesus spoke with such power and love.
They caught so many fish their boat was full
and their nets were breaking from the weight.

Simon knew this must be a man sent from God
and he fell to his knees there and then.
But Jesus said gently, "Come, follow me,
and I will make you fishers of men."

Simon and Andrew left lake, boat, and nets
to follow the Lord for the rest of their days.
Now Jesus asks YOU to "Come, follow me.
Come help me show EVERYONE
God's loving ways."

The Blind Man From Jericho

Bartimaeus was a blind man from Jericho.
He'd never seen a bluebird or a rainbow so bright.
But he could smell the flowers and touch the grass
and feel the warm sun rising after the night.

He would ask the Lord in his prayers each night,
"Please, let me see the lovely world you've made."
When morning came and his world was still dark
he'd wonder if God could hear when he prayed.

One day he was begging just outside of town
and he heard many people coming down the road.
"Move, you beggar, and let Jesus pass by!"
yelled a man who stepped out of the crowd.

Bartimaeus' heart skipped a beat or two
when he heard that the Son of God was near.
"Maybe he will answer my prayer," he thought,
and he called out loudly so Jesus would hear.

The crowd tried to hush him and push him aside,
but Bartimaeus continued to make his plea.
There on the roadside the blind beggar sat,
shouting "Jesus, son of David, have pity on me!"

Jesus stopped talking when Bartimaeus called.
"Call him over," he said to those who were near.
So they called Bartimaeus and told him, "Get up!
He is calling you. You have nothing to fear."

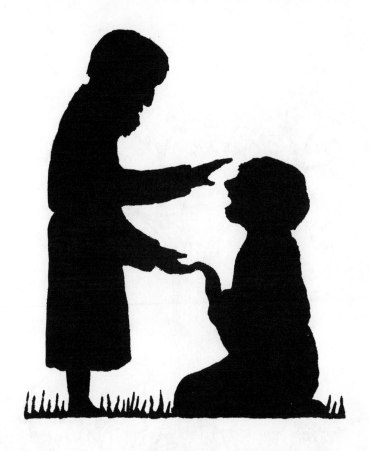

Now the poor, blind beggar was so eager to go
he threw off his old, ragged coat in his glee.
Jesus asked him, "What can I do for you?"
"Oh, Lord," said Bartimaeus, "I want to see!"

"Be on your way," Jesus told him then.
"Your faith has healed you" — and lo and behold!
Bartimaeus saw bluebirds and flowers and grass,
and, best of all, the loving face of the Lord.

Don't think that God doesn't know of your faith
or hear the words that you pray in the night.
Believe in his love and don't give up hope,
for to answer your prayer is his greatest delight.

Quintus the Brave

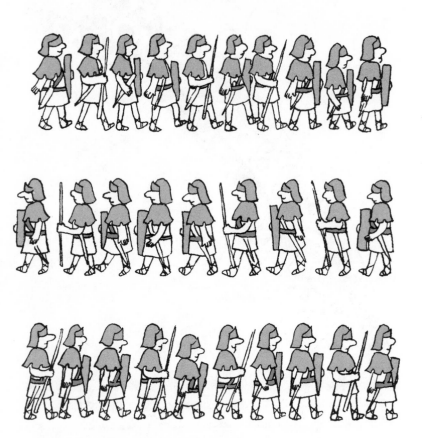

Quintus was a brave Roman soldier
with one hundred men at his call.
When Quintus said "March!"
one hundred men marched,
and they stopped at his "Halt"
one and all.

This commander of the great Roman army
had a young servant boy named Marc.
When the boy became ill,
Quintus went to seek help
for he loved him with all of his heart.

Now Quintus had heard about Jesus,
who healed body and soul with a word.
So he searched through the streets
and O'er high mountain peaks,
till he came upon Jesus, the Lord.

42

"Lord Jesus, my servant is hurting,
and he cannot move out of his bed."
Jesus turned to the brave young commander.
"I will come right away," he said.

"My Lord, I am not worthy
to have you come into my home.
But you, like myself,
have great power on earth.
Say the word and his pain will be gone."

Jesus turned to the crowd around him
saying, "Never have I seen such faith."
Then to Quintus he said,
"The boy has been healed.
Your faith has saved him from death."

44

No matter how big and strong you may get,
you will need the help that Jesus can bring.
Like Quintus the brave, always believe!
Faith in the Lord can do wonderful things.

Mary and Martha
of Bethany

There's a little house in Bethany
with smooth, white stones along the walk
and a cozy fireplace inside
and good friends gather there to talk.

This is the home of Mary and Martha,
sisters of the risen Lazarus.
One day when Jesus came to call,
Martha jumped up and began to fuss.

She took out the kettle and set it to boil,
and prepared all of Jesus' favorite treats:
wheat bread and honey, fish from the sea,
and spice cakes with tea, hot and sweet.

While Martha worked to prepare this feast,
Mary sat beside Jesus, so quietly,
listening to all that he had to say
about God and heaven and eternity.

"Lord," complained Martha, "can't you see
that Mary has left all the work to me?
Tell her to get up and do her share
of the good things I am doing for thee."

"Martha, Martha, you fidget and fuss
about all the work you say you must do.
Be quiet like Mary and hear my words,
for there's so much I want to say to you."

Like Martha, you have so much you must do,
such as helping others and learning to share,
but the very first thing Jesus asks of you
is to be quiet and sit with him in prayer.

Listen to his words when you go to church,
he wants to tell you that he cares for you.
Then go out and share and love and serve,
with Jesus to bless all the good that you do.

The Little Man in the Tree

In the beautiful city of Jericho
lived Zacchaeus, a rich and greedy fool.
A wee little man with a wee little heart,
who became wealthy by robbing the poor.

"Jesus is coming," he heard someone cry
outside his window one bright sunny morn.
Zacchaeus got dressed in his finest clothes
and set out to follow the crowd through town.

"I've just got to see this man Jesus,"
Zacchaeus thought as he trundled along.
But the crowd was so great and Zacchaeus so short,
he could not see beyond the noisy throng.

Zacchaeus elbowed and pushed to get ahead,
but the crowd pushed even harder than he.
He could tell that Jesus was coming near,
so he quickly climbed up a sycamore tree.

There in the branches of that sycamore tree
sat little Zaccheaus in his fancy pants.
Looking for Jesus to come down the road,
hoping to get just one little glance.

"Zacchaeus, come down," a voice gently called,
"for I plan to stay at your house this day."
Zacchaeus could hardly believe his ears,
it was JESUS who called him from the tree.

The rich little man welcomed Jesus with joy
and his own heart was changed by Jesus' love.
"I'll give half my belongings away," he said,
"and pay back more than I ever stole."

Just when you are looking for Jesus —
SURPRISE! He is already looking at you!
He calls you to welcome him into your heart
and he'll give you a love all shining and new.

55

Stephen,
the First Martyr

When Jesus had gone to the Father,
his apostles worked hand-in-hand
to spread the Word of his wonderful love
to cities and towns across the land.

God's Word was a beautiful thing to hear,
and the number who believed in Jesus grew.
"We must choose men," the apostles said,
"to help in the task that we are to do."

So they chose seven good and loyal men
to go out and preach about the Lord.
Then they prayed for God to bless the men,
and fill them with love for his holy Word.

One of these young men was called Stephen,
a beautiful young man of the faith.
Some say the face of Stephen would shine
like an angel come down to our earth.

When Stephen preached the Word of God,
his listeners believed without any doubt.
But some in the crowd didn't want to hear
of this Jesus that Stephen was talking about.

They ground their teeth in anger at him.
They shouted and picked up rocks and stones.
But Stephen looked up to heaven and saw
that he did not fight this battle alone.

"Look," he said, "I see in the sky,
Jesus standing at the right hand of God."
Then Stephen died with a heart full of love,
and rushed to the arms of his waiting Lord.

Stephen's words were silenced that day,
but his joy in Jesus lives on and on.
For that soul filled with grace,
  that beautiful face,
shines forth now in heaven
  for Father and Son.

Eager Saul
Who Became
Saint Paul

Saul of Tarsus was a hunter of great might.
He would stalk his prey both day and night.
He was there when Stephen died.
Because of him, God's people cried.
Because of him, they'd run and hide
   themselves from sight.

One morning Saul was on the road to town.
He was going out to hunt some Christians down.
He was struck by a blinding light
that took away his sight,
and a voice of power and might
    made a thundering sound.

"Saul, Saul," cried the voice
Saul heard that day.
"Why do you keep on hurting me this way?"
"Who are you?" Saul inquired,
his fearful heart afire.
"I am Jesus," said the voice,
  "whom you persecute today."

The love of God was born that day for Saul.
And we came to know him as Saint Paul.
He was a mighty hunter still,
hunting souls with which to fill
the Church that Jesus founded
   for us all.

By the same author . . .
THE ABC'S OF FAITH

Book One: God and You
The first book in the popular series written for children from preschool age to 8 or 9. Sections are entitled: God and You; Special Times of the Year; and God Made Our World.

Book Two: Following Jesus
This book includes sections: Following Jesus; Jesus' Friends: The Saints; and Jesus Teaches Us How to Live.

Book Three: The Ten Commandments
The third book of this series presents the Ten Commandments in words children understand, enjoy, and remember!

Book Four: The Seven Sacraments
This book centers on the sacraments and includes brief "sacrament prayers" for children.

Book Five: The Stories of Jesus
Delightfully illustrated, children will love these parables from the "Greatest Storyteller" of all time.

Book Six: Stories of God and His People from the Old Testament
God's Rainbow Promise, Jacob's Dream, and ten other stories from the Old Testament are tailor-made for young imaginations.

ABC'S OF THE ROSARY
Combines delightful poems and illustrations to create a refreshing way to help children understand and pray the rosary. Each of the fifteen mysteries are highlighted in the same charming style that has made the ABC's of Faith so popular.

Each 32-page booklet — $1.95

Order from your local bookstore or write to:
Liguori Publications, Box 060, Liguori, Missouri 63057
(Please add 50¢ postage and handling for first item ordered and 25¢ for each additional item.)